HALLEY IN 90 MINUTES

John and Mary Gribbin

HALLEY
(1656–1742)
in 90 minutes

Constable · London

First published in Great Britain 1997
by Constable and Company Limited
3 The Lanchesters, 162 Fulham Palace Road
London W6 9ER
Copyright © John and Mary Gribbin 1997
The right of John and Mary Gribbin to be identified
as authors of this work has been asserted by them
in accordance with the Copyright,
Designs and Patents Act 1988
ISBN 0 09 477030 1
Set in Linotype Sabon by
Rowland Phototypesetting Ltd,
Bury St Edmunds, Suffolk
Printed in Great Britain by
St Edmundsbury Press Ltd,
Bury St Edmunds, Suffolk

A CIP catalogue record of this book
is available from the British Library

Contents

ACKNOWLEDGEMENT

Thanks to Bill Murray, for help in tracking down reference material.

Halley in context

The first thing to get straight about Edmond Halley is his name. In the late seventeenth and early eighteenth centuries, spelling was partly a matter of personal taste, and different variations on both his first name and his surname survive in different documents. But the version he used himself on official documents (including his will) was definitely 'Edmond Halley', so we shall stick with that. The variations in the written versions of his surname are a useful guide to how that name was pronounced. Many people (including the diarist Samuel Pepys) just wrote the name down the way it sounded, without worrying about consistency in spelling at all, and from these phonetic variations on the theme it is clear that it was pronounced 'Hawley', so that the 'Hall' part of the surname rhymes with 'ball'.

This is not entirely a trivial point. Just as there was a certain *laissez-faire* attitude to spelling in those days – a lack of rigid rules to be obeyed, with the chosen spelling depending upon the whim of the writer – so the Universe, before Halley's time, was seen not as a place governed by rigid rules that had to be obeyed, but as one set up in accordance with the whim of the universal architect, God.

It had only been in the 1540s that Nicolaus Copernicus (carefully waiting until just before his death) had dared to publish the idea that the Sun, not the Earth, was at the centre of the Universe. Astronomy then promptly took a step backwards when Tycho Brahe (1546–1601) suggested that, while all the other planets move around the Sun, the Sun moves around the Earth, putting the Earth back at the centre of the Universe. But Tycho also took astronomy forward by making a series of superb observations of the movements of the planets across the sky, and these data were inherited by his assistant and successor as Imperial Mathematician to Rudolph II in Prague, Johannes Kepler (1571–1630).

Kepler had made his name at the end of the sixteenth century, when (using the Sun-centred Copernican system) he came up with what seemed to him a really neat idea: that the invisible spheres to which the six known planets were thought to be attached could be nested inside one another, just at the right relative distances, if they were fitted on either side of a nested set of the five 'perfect solids' (the tetrahedron, cube, octahedron, dodecahedron and icosahedron), like nested Russian dolls. It made a kind of sense – if that was the way God liked things, and if the orbits of the planets around the Sun were perfectly circular. There was a prejudice (going back to the Greeks) that the orbits had to be circular, because circles are perfect, and only perfection is good enough for the heavens.

But when Kepler, who was an able mathematician, got to grips with Tycho's data (especially the data for Mars), he found that planetary orbits are not circular, but elliptical. He worked out laws that describe the motion of a planet around the Sun (for example, that a planet moves faster when its elliptical orbit brings it closer to the Sun, in such a way that an imaginary line stretched from the Sun to the planet sweeps out equal areas in equal times), and began to change the view of the Universe from something set up at the whim of God to something obeying natural laws.

Galileo Galilei (1564–1642) was doing much the same thing at about the same time, over in Italy. He was explaining how pendulums swing, and how balls roll down inclined planes, in terms of natural laws which apply to all objects on Earth. He more or less invented the idea of doing experiments to test ideas about the way the world works, and used mathematics to describe the outcomes of those experiments. Between them, Kepler and Galileo set the scene for the entry of Isaac Newton (1642–1727), probably the greatest scientist who ever lived. Newton did two key things. First, he took the idea of experimentation further, placing it at the very centre of science. He once wrote to the Jesuit Ignace Gaston Pardies, in Paris:

> The best and safest method of philosophizing seems to be, first to enquire diligently into the properties of things, and to establish those properties by experiments and then to proceed more slowly to hypotheses for the explanation of them. For hypotheses should be employed only in explaining the properties of things, but not assumed in determining them; unless so far as they may furnish experiments.

In other words, don't *assume* that orbits are circular because you think circles are nice; *measure* the orbits and find out what shape they are!

It seems obvious to us, because that is the way science has been done since the time of Newton. But the idea of actually getting your hands dirty in experiments, instead of philosophizing in abstract terms about the way the Universe ought to be, was a revolutionary concept in the seventeenth century.

Newton's second great achievement was to show that the laws of physics which apply to swinging pendulums and balls rolling down planes here on Earth are *exactly the same* as the laws which apply in the Universe at large, holding planets in their orbits around the Sun. The most important thing about Newton's law of gravity is not that it is an 'inverse square law', interesting though that is, but that it is *universal*.

This is where Halley, a slightly younger contemporary of Newton's, comes in. As we shall see, Halley was instrumental in getting Newton to publish his ideas (he even paid for the cost of publishing Newton's famous book, the *Principia*). Halley also used Newton's law of gravity to predict the return of the comet that now bears Halley's name. The return of Halley's Comet in 1759, confirming Halley's prediction and Newton's laws, was the moment when science came of age. From then on, nobody could doubt that the world really is governed by universal laws which are describable in terms of mathematics.

But there was much more to Halley than the man who funded the publication of Newton's *Principia* and predicted the return of a certain comet. Even by the standards of his day, he was an extraordinary polymath – by turns, scientist, inventor and diplomat (almost certainly a spy for the British government); friend of Royalty, and sometime naval Captain; a man who left Oxford University without bothering to take his degree, and returned there in triumph as Savilian Professor of Geometry some thirty years later. You could almost argue that the thing Halley is most famous for today, predicting the return of his comet, is just about the least important thing he did, being in a sense merely a footnote to Newton's work.

But Halley doesn't deserve to be anybody's footnote. In truth, it is only compared with Newton that Halley seems anything other than a scientist of the first rank, one of the key people involved in the revolution that changed for ever the way we think about the Universe.

Life and work

Halley was born, according to his own account, on 29 October 1656 (this is on the Old Style Julian calendar still in use in England in those days; it corresponds to 8 November on the modern Gregorian calendar). We only have his word for it, because no record of his birth has ever been found – the relevant parish records may well have been destroyed in the Great Fire of London in 1666.

Some historians wonder whether Halley got the date right, because one surviving document shows that his father, a prosperous businessman and landlord also called Edmond Halley, married his mother, Anne Robinson, only seven weeks before the birth. We shouldn't necessarily jump to the obvious conclusion, though. This was during the period when England was ruled by Parliament (Charles I had been beheaded in 1649), and many couples were married first by the civil authorities, and only later (if at all) went through a church ceremony. It may well be that the proximity of the birth of their first child encouraged Edmond and Anne to back up their civil marriage with religious vows.

Young Edmond had a sister, Katherine, who was born in 1658 and died as a baby, and a brother, Humphrey, whose birth date is not known, but who died in 1684. As the sketchiness of these details shows, very little is known about his early life, and likewise very little is known about his private life in later years. Fortunately, a great deal is known about his public activities, especially where they are mentioned in the writings of his contemporaries (who included, as well as Samuel Pepys, John Evelyn).

What we do know is that the Halley family was well off when Edmond was young. One sign of this wealth is that Edmond Halley senior owned a country house three miles from the bustle of central London, in what is now Haggerston, part of the borough of Hackney, but was then a peaceful village. It was there that young Edmond was born. His father also owned a town house in Winchester Street (which has since disappeared under railway lines). The first sign of a decline in the family fortunes came with the Great Fire of 1666, which destroyed some of Halley senior's property, and reduced his income from rents. But his businesses – soap-boiling and salting – flourished in the late 1660s, and there were ample funds available for Edmond to be given the best available education, first at St Paul's School in London, and then at Oxford.

He obviously did well at school, and he was appointed school captain in 1671. He also developed his interest in astronomy. When he went up to Queen's College, Oxford, on 24 July 1673, he had a good knowledge of Latin, Greek and Hebrew, was a more than competent mathematician, knew the basics of navigation, and had developed some skill as an observational astronomer. His affluent background was a great help in pursuing his astronomical interests. He arrived in Oxford with a set of instruments, including a telescope 24 feet (7.3 m) long and a sextant two feet (60 cm) in diameter, that would have been the envy of many a pro-fessional contemporary astronomer.

There was one cloud on the horizon. Halley's mother had died in 1672. We don't know exactly where, when or why, but she was buried on 24 October that year. As we shall see, his mother's death would come to have a profound impact on Edmond as a consequence of his father's unfortunate second marriage.

Science, and astronomy in particular, was beginning to take off in England, helped by sponsorship from high places. The Restoration of the monarchy in 1660 had brought Charles II to the throne; what became the Royal Society (the oldest scientific institution in the world with an unbroken existence) was also founded in 1660, and received its Charter in 1663. Interest in science in the explosively heady years of the Restoration, the need for better methods of navigation for the growing navy, and royal patronage soon led to the foundation of the Royal Greenwich Observatory and the appointment of John Flamsteed (1646–1719) as the first Astronomer Royal, in 1675.

That year, Halley, as an 18-year-old Oxford undergraduate, wrote to Flamsteed. He described some results of his astronomical observations which seemed to suggest that published tables of astronomical data were wrong, and politely asked if Flamsteed could confirm that Halley's numbers were correct. In due course, Halley would succeed Flamsteed as Astronomer Royal. The correspondence between the two of them that began in 1675 was an important step towards that appointment, and it was with Flamsteed's encouragement that Halley wrote his first scientific paper (about planetary orbits) later in 1675, while still an undergraduate. It was published the following year.

Halley was by all accounts an outstandingly able student, and would surely have passed his degree with flying colours. But he became impatient to build on the success of his early work, and to make a name for himself as Flamsteed and others were doing. Flamsteed was making a catalogue of the positions of the stars, using the improved telescopes that were becoming available, which made his measurements far more accurate than those in older catalogues obtained with more primitive sighting instruments – using 'open sights'.

Halley hit on the scheme of doing the same

kind of thing for the stars of the southern sky, from the outpost of St Helena in the South Atlantic, at that time the most southerly British outpost. His father supported the idea to the tune of offering Halley an allowance of £300 a year (three times Flamsteed's salary as Astronomer Royal). With Flamsteed acting as a supportive intermediary, the scheme was put to the government and to the king, who 'recommended' to the East India Company that the young man and a friend, James Clerke, be given passage to St Helena, which the company controlled. They sailed in November 1676 – the degree, for the moment, forgotten. Halley was just 20.

With severe weather to contend with, the catalogue took more than a year to complete. Halley also observed a transit of the planet Mercury across the Sun's disc, on 28 October 1677, and carried out other scientific studies while he was there. But there was also time for other activities. Hints of sexual impropriety followed Halley throughout his early adult life, starting with his visit to St Helena. The antiquarian John Aubrey (1626–1697) alludes in his *Brief Lives* (not published until long after Aubrey's death) to a long-married but childless couple who travelled out to St Helena in the same ship as Halley, and remarks that 'before he came [home] from the Island, she was brought to bed of a Child'.

Whatever the truth of the rumours, they had no effect on Halley's career. He returned from the South Atlantic in the spring of 1678 in something of a triumph, and his *Catalogue of the Southern Stars* was published in November that year, earning him the sobriquet 'Our Southern Tycho' from Flamsteed himself. There was also another small matter that needed to be put right. Halley's work was clearly more than good enough to justify him being awarded a degree, but the rules at Oxford were strict – he had not stayed up for the minimum number of terms required, whatever his intellectual merits. At the suggestion of Sir Joseph Williamson, the Secretary of State (who had been instrumental in obtaining approval for the St Helena expedition), the king wrote to the Vice Chancellor of Oxford 'recommending [Halley] for the degree of M.A. without any condition of performing any previous or subsequent exercises for the same.'

It may or may not have helped that Halley had tactfully named a group of southern stars as a new constellation, *Robur Carolinum*, in honour of the famous oak tree in which Charles II had once hidden. He received the degree on 3 December, just three days after being elected a Fellow of the Royal Society. His friends now included, as well as Flamsteed, Robert Hooke and other leading lights in that Society. His next task was to visit the German astronomer Johannes Hevelius (1611–1687), in Danzig, as a representative of the Royal Society itself. Not bad for an undergraduate drop-out!

This was a mission requiring tact. Hevelius was an old man who clung to the old method of observing star positions with 'open sights', and claimed incredible accuracy for his results. The Royal Society wanted to set the matter straight – not out of malice, but for scientific reasons. Could the old astronomer's data be trusted or not? Halley went to find out. He reported back that, indeed, everything was fine, and Hevelius really had been achieving the accuracy he claimed. But there was more to this than meets the eye. In a letter to a friend, Halley later claimed that he had been kind to Hevelius because he was worried that if he were honest it might hasten the death of 'an old peevish Gentleman,' and later still he remarked 'I would not hasten his departure by exposing him and his observations.' But even this may have been an excuse.

Hevelius's first wife had died in 1662, and in 1663 he had married Elisabetha, the beautiful 16-year-old daughter of a rich merchant (in 1663, Hevelius was 52). When Halley visited Danzig in 1679, Elisabetha was still only 32, and a known beauty; Hevelius was 68; Halley was a vigorous young man in his 23rd year; the rest is rumour and innuendo (but plenty of it, at the time and subsequently).

Whatever the reason, the fact that Halley reported favourably on Hevelius's open-sights observations, and that it soon became clear that they were not in fact as good as he claimed, contributed to a rift between Halley and Flamsteed which was never healed. It is possible that Flamsteed, a very serious-minded man, first took exception to the rumours about Halley and Elisabetha Hevelius. The way in which the quarrel unfolded no doubt owed much to the fact that Flamsteed's former protégé soon began to outdo the Astronomer Royal himself.

But Halley did not hasten to develop his career in science. Still comfortably supported by the allowance from his father, for just over a year he divided his time between Oxford and London, attending meetings of the Royal Society and (as we know from the papers of his contemporaries) visiting one of the capital's fashionable coffee houses, Jonathan's, in Change Alley. At the end of this period, in the winter of 1680–81, a bright comet appeared and became a major talking-point, not just among astronomers. First seen in November 1680, the comet was observed moving towards the Sun, and was then lost in the Sun's glare; a little later, it was seen moving away from the Sun. It became the brightest comet that anyone alive at the time had witnessed, clearly visible from the streets of cities like London and Paris in those days before artificial lighting.

But this was before Newton published his work on gravity, and most people thought that they had seen two different comets, one moving towards the Sun and another moving away. Comets were still mysterious and inexplicable heavenly phenomena. Although Flamsteed was one of the few people who suggested that this might have been one object moving first towards and then away from the Sun, he had no inkling that it was in an orbit around the Sun, and thought that its motion had been reversed by magnetic repulsion.

Halley saw the 'first' comet from London at the end of 1680, just before he set off on his Grand Tour of Europe, accompanied by a friend, Robert Nelson, the son of another rich London businessman. This tour of France and Italy, featuring visits to Paris and Rome, was the social thing to do for rich young gentlemen (and, indeed, ladies), but Halley wanted to meet astronomers and other men of learning on the Continent. One of the main topics of conversation among both scientists and other people in the early part of their journey was the 'second' comet. Among the people Halley discussed it with was Giovanni

Cassini, head of the Paris Observatory, who was the first to suggest that the rings of Saturn are made up of a myriad of tiny particles, orbiting Saturn like miniature moons.

The Tour took in many of the cities of France and Italy on its way to Rome, where Nelson stayed and found love, marrying the second daughter of the Earl of Berkeley. Halley came back to England by a more circuitous route than he had followed to Rome, talking in Holland as well as Paris. He was back in London on 24 January 1682, having, in the words of Aubrey, 'contracted an acquaintance and friendship with all the eminentest mathematicians in France and Italy.'

At this point, the lack of details about Halley's private life becomes frustrating. Although his trip around Europe seems leisurely by today's standards, he actually spent only a few weeks more than a year abroad, quite short for a Grand Tour in those days. We know that his father remarried at about this time, though we don't know exactly when, and it is possible that Halley hurried back to attend the wedding. Whatever, on 20 April 1682 – and completely out of the blue, as far as any surviving historical records are concerned – Halley, now 25, himself got married, to Mary Tooke, the daughter of an officer at the Exchequer (there is some uncertainty about his exact post). The wedding took place at St James' Church, in Duke Place, not far from the Winchester Street home of Halley's father.

What little we know of Halley's married life can all be presented in one short paragraph. The couple were together for more than fifty years, and seem to have been very happy with each other the whole time. They had three children: Edmond (who was born in 1698, became a surgeon in the navy, and died shortly before his father), and two daughters, both born in 1688 but not twins – Margaret (who never married) and Catherine (who married twice). There may have been other offspring who died in infancy (there usually were, in those days). And that's it.

Edmond and Mary Halley set up home in Islington, then a village just to the north of London, where he set up a small but well-equipped private observatory. Halley, still funded by his father, was an active observer, publishing papers on the motion of the Moon, on Saturn and one of its moons, Rhea, and on the tides; he also played an important part in the activities of the Royal Society. He became interested in the idea that variations in the magnetism of the Earth from place to place could be used as an aid to navigation – indeed, he had made magnetic observations on his voyages to and from St Helena. And he was also keenly interested in another bright comet that appeared in the skies in 1682.

That was the year in which William Penn, a Fellow of the Royal Society and a friend of Halley, set out to found the Pennsylvania Colony. It was also the most intense period of cold in what has become known as the Little Ice Age; in the winter of 1683–4 the Thames at London was covered with a layer of ice 25 cm thick, and a tented 'Frost Fair' was set up on the frozen river. It was this historical freeze-up that formed the basis for the severe fictional winter weather described much later in *Lorna Doone*.

At the end of that winter, Halley's life changed. On Wednesday, 5 March 1684, his father went out and never returned. Five days later, his unclothed body was found by the river at Temple Farm. The resulting inquest returned a verdict of murder.

Partly because of the loss of income following the Great Fire, and partly because of the extravagance of his second wife, the older Edmond's fortune had been considerably diminished, and what was left of it became the subject of a long and expensive legal battle between his widow and his son. The younger Edmond did not become a pauper overnight (almost certainly, his wife had brought a reasonable dowry with her), but he could no longer rely on the secure and generous support he had had throughout his career. Less than two years later, in January 1686, he had to resign his cherished Fellowship of the Royal Society in order to take up the paid post of Clerk to the Society – paid servants were not allowed to be Fellows. It is hard to escape the conclusion that by then Halley was, if not exactly desperate for an income, then certainly in a quite different financial situation from the days when he could rely on an annual allowance three times the salary of the Astronomer Royal. But it was in the period between the death of his father and his appointment as Clerk to the Royal Society that Halley made one of the most significant friendships of his life, when he visited Isaac Newton in Cambridge.

Newton and Halley had already corresponded about the comet of 1682, and it is possible that they met briefly that year on one of Newton's visits to London. At that time, though, Newton very much kept himself to himself, and took little part in the activities of the Royal Society, having argued bitterly with Robert Hooke, the Secretary of the Society, about his theory of light. What brought Halley and Newton together in 1684 was a growing interest among many astronomers in *why* the orbits of the planets around the Sun should obey Kepler's laws.

Halley became interested in the problem. He realized that Kepler's law relating the time it takes a planet to go round the Sun to the distance of that planet from the Sun could be explained if there was a force of attraction between the Sun and the planet which went as one over the square of the distance between them. That is, the force is four times less if the distance is doubled, nine times less if the distance is trebled, and so on – the famous 'inverse square' law.

But this was only an educated guess. Halley looked at the numbers, guessed a pattern which they would fit, and found that they did fit that pattern. For all he knew, though, it might be a coincidence – one could imagine a planet in an orbit which did not obey the inverse square law. And there was no proof that an inverse square law must always produce elliptical orbits.

Halley mentioned his discovery to Hooke, who said that not only had he already reached the same conclusion, but that he could prove it, using geometry. But he refused to divulge the secret! (Hooke was a very strange man who regularly tried to claim priority for ideas other people invented, but that is another story.) Infuriated by Hooke's attitude, and suspecting that he did not really have the proof, Halley went off to Cambridge in August 1684 to discuss the puzzle with Newton, already renowned as a skilled mathematician.

The best contemporary account of what

happened when 'Dr Halley' visited Cambridge comes from Newton's mathematician friend Abraham De Moivre (1667–1754), a French Huguenot refugee:

> After they had been some time together, the Dr asked him [Newton] what he thought the Curve would be that would be described by the Planets supposing the force towards the Sun to be reciprocal to the square of their distances from it. Sir Isaac replied immediately that it would be an Ellipsis, the Doctor struck with joy & amazement asked him how he knew it, why saith he I have calculated it, whereupon Dr Halley asked him for his calculation without any farther delay.

Newton rummaged in his papers, but claimed not to be able to lay hands on the proof. He may just have been playing for time, still cautious about going public with his ideas and risking another public argument with the likes of Hooke. But he promised to work out the proof again, and send it on to Halley in London. He was as good as his word – better, in fact, for in two months' time Halley held in his hands a nine-page paper from Newton which elegantly explained the mathematical basis for all of Kepler's laws, using the inverse square formulation of the law of gravity.

It was clear that this was just the tip of an iceberg of unpublished work, and Halley went back to Cambridge to find out just how much Newton had still hidden up his sleeve. It was on this trip that he persuaded Newton to write what became his famous book, the *Principia*. In it, Newton would explain how gravity not just holds the planets in their orbits around the Sun, but holds the Moon in orbit around the Earth, and explains the fall of an apple from a tree. He would put forward his three laws of motion, and lay the basis of a system of mechanics that would remain unchallenged until Albert Einstein came along. This so-called Newtonian mechanics still provides the basis for everyday needs, and is used, for example, to calculate the construction of a bridge or the flight-path of a spaceprobe to its intended destination.

Halley reported back to the Royal Society on 19 December 1684, with the news that

Newton had promised to publish his results, and would send the mathematical proofs to the Society in due course. It took Newton well over a year to complete his epic, constantly encouraged by Halley, who provided comments on the various drafts as the work progressed, and eventually took on the responsibility for reading the proofs.

It was during this period that Halley's own situation changed and he became Clerk to the Society. He had already moved house, to Golden Lion Court in Aldersgate Street, in 1685; so he was conveniently located for the Society's meetings. The Society waived its stipulation that its Clerk should be a single man and live in Gresham College, where meetings took place. Whatever his reasons for taking up the post (and the need for an income must have been one of them), this was good news for Newton. Halley was a diligent and efficient Clerk, who did much to ensure the smooth running of the Society's affairs, while continuing with his own research. The first part of the *Principia* was delivered in April 1686, and though the details are vague it seems clear that Halley was instrumental in ensuring that on 19 May the Society ordered that it should be printed at its own expense (incidentally, the Society's President at the time was Samuel Pepys).

Unfortunately, the Society was not able to live up to its promise. A little earlier, what meagre funds there were available were used to pay for the publication of Francis Willughby's *History of Fishes*. It proved virtually unsaleable – there were still copies in the Society's inventory of 1743 – and with no money to hand, instead of paying Halley his £50 salary that year the Society gave him 50 copies of Willughby's book! There was certainly no money to hand for the publication of Newton's book, and Halley had very little choice but to make good the promise by funding the publication himself (so he cannot have been completely impoverished during his time as Clerk). There is, though, a happy ending: unlike the fish book, the *Principia* was a modest success, selling reasonably well, and Halley made a tiny profit out of it. He certainly earned it.

As Newton had feared, even before the publication of his work there erupted another row with Hooke about priority, and Newton threatened to withdraw his work from publication. It fell to Halley to tell Hooke to put up or shut up – either produce his claimed independent proof of the inverse square law, or let the matter rest. Hooke never did back up his claims, and Newton was soothed sufficiently to allow the publication to go ahead as planned. The book appeared in July 1687. It changed forever the way people thought about the world, and its publication marked the birth of modern science. A copy of the first edition was presented to the new king, James II, who had succeeded Charles II in 1685. This was the beginning of a turbulent time in English politics, as the Catholic James II was shortly (in 1689) replaced by the Protestant William and Mary; none of this deeply concerned Halley, who is reported as saying:

For my part, I am for the King in possession. If I am protected, I am content. I am sure we pay dear enough for our Protection, & why should we not have the Benefit of it?

Such diplomacy would soon be put to good use.

In the late 1680s and early 1690s, while still working diligently as Clerk to the Royal Society, Halley published a series of scientific papers and discussed other ideas at the Society's meetings. These included mathematical papers (he was always good at maths), various astronomical studies, and an investigation of the possible causes of the Biblical flood. This last piece of work was to have an almost immediate adverse effect on his career. In those days, the Church accepted the Biblical chronology which, counting back the generations (all the 'begats') listed in the Bible from Jesus to Adam, yielded a date of 4004 BC for the creation of the Earth. (If you want to be precise, John Lightfoot, Vice-Chancellor of the University of Cambridge, had declared, following the publication of Archbishop Ussher's *Sacred Chronology* in 1620, that Adam had been created at 9 a.m. on Sunday, 23 October 4004 BC.) Halley realized that the kind of dramatic changes in the features of the Earth associated with an event on the scale of the Flood implied a much longer history.

He accepted that there was some basis of fact in the Biblical story, but in trying to put this on a scientific footing he ran into conflict with traditional Churchmen by suggesting a very much greater age for the Earth than they were willing to countenance. When he tried to estimate the Earth's age by analysing the saltiness of the sea, he came up with a similarly long timescale.

Ever since his voyage to St Helena, he had maintained an interest in the sea and in the workings of the ocean and atmosphere. He was intrigued by the idea of using magnetic variations to measure the position of a ship at sea (which led him to develop one of the first theories of terrestrial magnetism), and he was interested too in the way the wind blows. He found the law which relates the change in the pressure of the atmosphere to height above sea level, and in 1686 he published a paper on the trade winds and monsoons, which included the first meteorological chart, a map showing wind patterns around the world. But Halley was also very much a practical man, and at the beginning of the 1690s he was off to Pagham, in Sussex, where he carried out experiments in deep sea diving, using a frigate provided by the Admiralty. Halley invented a practical diving-bell, which enabled men to work on the seabed in a depth of ten fathoms (18 m) for up to two hours at a time. And, being a good scientist, while he was at it he carried out experiments on the behaviour of sound and light under water.

In 1691, Halley published a paper explaining how observations of a transit of Venus (the passage of the planet in front of the Sun's disc) could be used to measure the distance to the Sun. Because of the geometry of the orbits of the Earth and Venus, these transits are rare events, occurring in pairs (with the two transits in each pair about 8 years apart) at intervals of more than a century. Halley showed how observers at widely separated places on Earth would see the transit slightly differently, because of parallax. (To see parallax at work, hold up one finger at arm's length and watch how it seems to move when you close each of your eyes alternately.) By comparing their observations, the results from the two teams and the geometry of the Earth–

Venus–Sun alignment could be used to work out the distance to the Sun.

Halley would return to this theme in 1716, when he predicted that the next pair of transits of Venus would occur in 1761 and 1769. He wrote:

I strongly urge diligent searchers of the heavens (for whom, when I have ended my days, these sights are being kept in store) to bear in mind this injunction of mine and to apply themselves actively and with all their might to making the necessary observations.

But a lot of water would flow under the bridge before he published that paper.

Even allowing for the role of amateurs and gentlemen of independent means in science in the seventeenth century, it is amazing that such an outpouring of work could come from a man who was still only the Clerk to the Royal Society. Halley himself chafed at this limitation, and was eager to establish himself in a more important academic position. The opportunity seemed to present itself in June

1691, when he was carrying out his diving experiments at Pagham and heard that Edward Bernard, the Savilian Professor of Astronomy at Oxford University, had resigned his post. Halley thought that he had a good chance of filling the vacancy, and put his name forward. But there was a snag. The appointment was subject to the approval of the Church authorities, and Halley's views on the age of the Earth had caused him to be regarded a heretic. In a letter to a friend, Abraham Hill, he expressed his concern that he might not get the post, 'there being a caveat entered against me, till I can show that I am not guilty of asserting the eternity of the world.'

He was right. Partly for his heretical views, and partly because of the opposition of Flamsteed (by now, Flamsteed and Halley were firm foes, though the exact reasons for their falling out are not known), he didn't get the job, which went to David Gregory (1661–1708), one of Newton's protégés.

It looked as if the doors of academe were closed against Halley. But for a man who, when circumstances required it, had been willing to resign his Fellowship of the Royal Society in order to work as a humble Clerk, there were always other options. Of course, his scientific work continued, in all its diversity – it was in March 1693, for example, that he presented his calculated tables of human mortality, the first scientific basis for life assurance, to the Royal Society.

Also in 1693, together with a friend, Benjamin Middleton (about whom very little is known), Halley made a formal proposal to the Admiralty requesting that a ship be provided for a voyage of scientific investigation. No papers survive to reveal exactly what they intended to investigate, but it is clear that Middleton was at first the leading light in the project, since Robert Hooke's diary (in his entry for 11 January 1693) records that Halley had spoken 'of going in Middleton's ship to discover,' although tantalizingly Hooke does not tell us what it was they hoped to discover! Clearly, though, from the outset at least one of the aims was to find ways to improve navigation at sea, something of huge importance to the navy, and amply justifying the loan of a ship.

The proposal met with such an enthusiastic response from the Admiralty that (by order of Queen Mary II) a small ship was specially built at Deptford for the proposed expedition. It was of a kind known as a pink, developed in the Netherlands, with three masts, bulging sides and a flat bottom, designed for carrying stores and navigating in shallow waters. The vessel was launched on 1 April 1694, and named the *Paramore*; she was 52 feet long, 18 feet wide at the beam, had a draught of 9 feet 7 inches, and displaced 89 tons.Try pacing out those dimensions (16 m by 5.5 m) in the garden and see if you would fancy voyaging to the South Atlantic in her.

There was a delay of nearly two years before anything more is heard of the project. Halley went about his work as Clerk to the Royal Society, and continued to carry out his own scientific studies. But nothing is heard of Middleton, and the delay may have been caused by him. By 1696, though, the expedition had clearly become Halley's affair, so much so that on 4 June that year he received a Royal Commission from William III (Mary had died on 28 December 1694) appointing him as Master and Commander of the *Paramore*. In other words, Halley, a landsman, had been appointed as captain of a king's ship in the Royal Navy – the only landsman ever to receive such a commission.

There was a reason for this. At the time, the expedition was seen as being the responsibility of the Royal Society, a private voyage using a ship borrowed from the navy (even though that ship had been specially built for the job). So it was clear that Halley should be in charge. But to ensure discipline, it was intended that the crew should be provided by the navy, with the normal chain of command. The costs of the expedition would be the responsibility of the Society, and Sir John Hoskins, the Society's fourth President, handsomely provided a bond of £600 for the purpose. On 19 June 1696, the Navy Board received a letter from Halley detailing the ship's company of 15 men, 2 boys, himself, 'Mr Middleton and his servant', making 20 in all. This is the last we hear of Middleton. But on the brink of setting sail, the expedition suffered another delay, and in August 1696 the *Paramore* was laid up in wet dock. This time, the delay was caused by another twist in Halley's career.

Throughout 1695, Halley's main scientific interest had been comets. From studies of historical records he showed that at least some comets followed elliptical orbits, obeying the same laws as planets in their movement around the Sun, and he exchanged a stream of letters with Newton on the subject. He was also keenly interested in the comet he had seen (along with many other people) in 1682, and had begun to suspect that it had been seen at least three times before, and was in an orbit around the Sun with a period of 75 or 76 years.

But none of this was published in the mid-1690s. Halley knew that Flamsteed had made accurate observations of this comet, and needed those data to check his theory, but Flamsteed was not on speaking terms with Halley. Flamsteed was, though, on quite good terms with Newton (somewhat ironically, since Newton was seldom on good terms with anyone for long), and Halley hoped that Newton could get the observations from Flamsteed and pass them on to him. It is, incidentally, in a letter from Flamsteed to Newton, dated 7 February 1695, that we get a hint of why Flamsteed had taken against Halley: he writes that Halley has 'almost ruined himself by his indiscreet behaviour,' and alludes to deeds 'too foule and large for [discussion in] a letter.'

By 1696 Halley and Newton were firm friends, with a common interest in comets. Newton was well aware of how much he owed Halley in getting the *Principia* published, and may have felt slightly guilty about having supported Gregory's application for the Oxford job instead of Halley's. In 1696, Newton was appointed Warden of the Royal Mint, and given the task of overseeing a much needed reform of the currency. He was so successful that three years later he was made Master of the Mint, and never returned to scientific research. But one of his first acts as Warden was to appoint Halley, in the late summer of 1696, as Deputy Comptroller of the subsidiary Mint at Chester.

This was always going to be a temporary job to see the reform of the currency through, and obviously Newton thought he was doing

Halley a favour by providing him with an income, if only £90 per annum and only for a couple of years. Unfortunately, Halley did not enjoy his time at the Mint in Chester. He met with insubordination and resistance to his attempts to eradicate dishonest practices (it was all too easy for staff to line their own pockets). He did, as ever, carry out many scientific observations during his time there (including a study of the local variation in the Earth's magnetic field), and he continued to act as Clerk to the Royal Society, though for the first time this work suffered because of his other commitments. Newton knew that Halley was unhappy at Chester, and offered to find him other posts on more than one occasion; but Halley stuck it out until the regional mints were closed down in 1698, when he returned to London.

Now, there was no need to delay the voyage in the *Paramore* any longer. Official enthusiasm for the expedition had increased so much that the ship was to sail as a Royal Navy vessel, under the patronage of William III, at no cost to the Royal Society. As a naval ship, the *Paramore* had guns and a navy crew. But no question seems to have been raised about Halley's appointment, and he remained Master and Commander. On 15 October 1698 he was issued with instructions for a year-long voyage aimed at measuring magnetic variations and thereby providing a method of navigation. (The instructions came as no surprise to Halley; he had drafted them, and given them to the Admiralty, which then passed them back to him as orders.) But before the ship set sail, Halley had a chance to meet Tsar Peter the Great (1672–1725), who was visiting England to study English shipbuilding practice with a view to modernizing the Russian navy.

Peter stayed in Deptford for a time, literally getting his hands dirty (and calloused) as he studied how ships were built there. His heavy drinking, womanizing and crude manners became the stuff of many stories, and he and his entourage wrecked John Evelyn's house, which they had borrowed. There are hazy anecdotal accounts that Halley dined with the tsar on more than one occasion, and joined in some of the wilder games, which included being pushed in a wheelbarrow through the ornamental hedges of the garden. When Peter left, the Exchequer was obliged to pay Evelyn £300 in compensation for all the damage, including the cost of three broken wheelbarrows. This total sum is put into perspective by comparing it with the expected cost of the twelve-month voyage of the *Paramore*, which was no more than £600. Clearly, if Halley was a friend of Tsar Peter, it is easy to see why he was no friend of the prim and proper Flamsteed.

The *Paramore* set off on its voyage on 20 October 1698. Halley the sea captain was a few days short of his 42nd birthday, and about to have his authority tested in no uncertain fashion. You might think that as a landsman entrusted with a king's ship, Halley would have been given a First Lieutenant he could rely on, a hand-picked trusty seafarer who could look after the actual running of the ship. Not a bit of it. Somehow, through indifference or carelessness, or both, the Admiralty managed to saddle Halley with one Edward Harrison, a fine seaman and competent officer with eight years' service, who just happened to bear a grudge against the

Royal Society in general and Halley in particular.

In 1694, Harrison had submitted a paper on the longitude problem to the Society, and had it rejected. In 1696, Harrison published his ideas in a little book, and the Admiralty appointed a committee of experts, including Halley, to look into it. The committee decided that Harrison's ideas were worthless. So in addition to the natural unhappiness any career naval officer might have felt at being ordered to serve under a landsman, Harrison had every incentive to show Halley up as an unsuitable commander and an incompetent navigator – he may even have engineered his own appointment for that purpose.

In spite of the difficulties caused by Harrison, which were carefully kept short of open disobedience to orders, the *Paramore* reached Brazil and the West Indies and carried out some of Halley's planned scientific work. (The voyage was eventful in other ways: the *Paramore* was fired upon by an English merchantman, mistaking it for a pirate vessel.) But in April and May of 1699, in the West Indies, matters came to such a head that

Halley decided to cut the voyage short and head home. Reading between the lines, Harrison seems to have said something to the effect that 'if you think you're a real captain, you can bloody well navigate the ship home yourself,' and stomped off to his bunk. To Harrison's undoubted chagrin, Halley navigated the ship home perfectly (proving that if you want a good navigator you should hire an astronomer). In England, Harrison was court-martialled, but escaped with a reprimand since there was no proof that he had disobeyed a direct order. If nothing else, the whole episode sheds some light on Halley's powerful personality and determination; not a man to get in the way of.

Halley took advantage of the brief time he spent back in England to resign his post as Clerk to the Royal Society, and set off again in the *Paramore*, now in unquestioned command, on 16 September 1699 (the first voyage had ended on 28 June). He carried out magnetic observations all the way down to latitude 52° South (almost level with the tip of South America), encountering huge icebergs. He also made meteorological observations, and carried out important charting work. The ship returned to Plymouth, in good order, on 27 August 1700. (If you want to know more about Halley's voyages, see *The Three Voyages of Edmond Halley*, edited by Norman Thrower, Hakluyt Society, London, 1980.)

As with his first ever voyage, his return was a triumph. As well as reporting to the Admiralty and publishing charts of his voyages, Halley presented papers on his discoveries made on the two *Paramore* voyages to the Royal Society (to which he was re-elected as a Fellow in 1700), and was on the point of resuming his career as a scientist, but without the time-consuming duties of the Clerkship. However, in 1701 he asked to borrow a ship from the Admiralty for a study of the tides in the English Channel. They responded with alacrity, giving him command of the *Paramore* again, and he set out on 14 June that year, completing his work and paying off the crew of the pink on 16 October. (Nobody except Halley ever commanded the *Paramore* on a lengthy voyage; in 1706 she was sold for £122.) But there was a hidden agenda for this last voyage: as well as the genuine scientific work, Halley, under orders from the Admiralty, carried out some clandestine surveying of French ports and harbour approaches, for use in case of war.

The powers that be were obviously pleased by the discreet way in which Halley carried out this work, and in 1702, after Queen Anne succeeded William III, Halley was sent as an envoy to Vienna, to advise the Austrian Emperor on harbour fortifications in the Adriatic. He returned on a second mission to check that the work was being carried out properly (his advice must have been good, since Emperor Leopold presented him with a valuable diamond ring as a reward). Both trips, which involved extensive travel across Europe and meetings with many eminent people – including, on the second trip, dinner in Hanover with the future King George I of England and his son – seem to have been used as cover for a little spying. He returned to England in November 1703, and a letter dated 14 January 1704 from the Earl of Nottingham instructs the Chancellor of the Exchequer to pay the sum of £36 for Halley's expenses 'out of the secret service'.

What was there left for the scientist, sailor and spy to achieve? Only his dearest wish – an academic post. He had failed twelve years earlier to get the chair of astronomy but on 28 October 1703, just before Halley returned from his second diplomatic mission across Europe, John Wallis, the Savilian Professor of Geometry at Oxford, died. Who else but Halley could replace him? He still had his opponents, notably Flamsteed (who wrote in a letter to Abraham Sharp dated 18 December 1703 that Halley 'now talks, swears, and drinks brandy like a sea captain' – which, after all, he was), but he had far more supporters, and was at the height of his fame. At the end of November 1703, Halley was elected to the Council of the Royal Society, the same day that Newton became its President, and in 1704, at the age of 47, he was duly appointed to the Professorship in Oxford. To his delight, around Oxford he was generally referred to as 'Captain Halley', at least until 1710, when he received the degree of Doctor of Civil Law from Oxford and became 'Doctor Halley' to all. (It's interesting that this seems at that time to have been regarded as a more important title than 'Professor'.)

Once he had become a respectable, and respected, academic, Professor Halley's life was relatively uninteresting. There were no more deep-sea diving, naval voyages or spying expeditions. His book *A Synopsis of the Astronomy of Comets*, largely based on the work he had done ten years earlier, was published in 1705, and included the famous prediction of the return of the comet of 1682, which Halley suggested would occur 'about the year 1758,' almost certainly long after Halley himself would be dead. During his time in Oxford, Halley studied (among other things) eclipses, meteors and the aurora, as well as doing important work in mathematics; but his most important contribution (apart from his theory of comets) was in stellar astronomy. This harked back to his first major piece of work, the map of the southern skies; there was also an unfortunate episode involving Flamsteed's observations.

The Royal Greenwich Observatory had been set up expressly so that Flamsteed could prepare more accurate astronomical tables to improve navigation, but he was extremely reluctant to publish, and kept his results to himself. He claimed that though he was paid by the Crown, this was only a token sum, and since most of the cost of the instruments at the Observatory and the observing itself had been met from his own pocket, he was entitled to regard the observational results as his own property, to be published only when he was good and ready, and not before. In Flamsteed's defence, this was partly because he was a perfectionist who wanted to dot every *i* and cross every *t* before showing his catalogue to the world. In 1704, Newton, as President of the Royal Society, had persuaded Flamsteed to hand over some of his data, and over the next few years the printing of a new star catalogue was begun. But the operation ground to a halt in the face of Flamsteed's continuing prevarication. By 1710 everybody had had enough, and Queen Anne issued a Royal Warrant appointing Newton and such other Fellows of the Royal Society as he chose to act as a Board of Visitors to the Observatory. The Board had the authority to demand all of Flamsteed's results so far, and to have a fair copy of his continuing annual observations within six months of the end of each year. Even Flamsteed couldn't argue with a Royal Warrant, and Newton gave Halley the task of collecting together the raw material from Flamsteed, including his old data from 1704, and knocking it into shape for publication.

Halley had to add a lot of data of his own to fill gaps in the material supplied by Flamsteed, and this effort renewed his interest in making accurate observations of the positions of the stars. He made every effort to get Flamsteed to cooperate in the project, including sending him the proofs for checking, but without success. The Flamsteed saga wore on – the version of the catalogue edited by Halley appeared in 1712 under the title *Historia coelestis Brittanica*, and eventually Flamsteed (now in his late sixties) and his wife managed to buy up most of the copies that were printed and burn them. The episode did, however, encourage him to put his data into a form he was happy with, and though the resulting catalogue was not published until 1725, six years after Flamsteed's death, it gave nearly three thousand star positions to an accuracy of 10 arc seconds, a great improvement over earlier catalogues.

Meanwhile, from around the time he began work on Flamsteed's data, Halley carefully investigated the data in a star catalogue included in Ptolemy's astronomical compendium the *Almagest* and based on material originally gathered by Hipparchus in the second century BC. Halley found that most of the star positions given in the old catalogue closely matched observations made in his time, but a few were significantly different from the positions seen in the eighteenth-century sky. Because most of the positions did agree with his contemporary data, Halley realized that the few 'errors' were not observational mistakes, and that these stars had actually moved across the sky since the time of Hipparchus. The star Arcturus, for example, appeared in the early eighteenth century twice the width of the full Moon (more than a degree) from the position recorded by Ptolemy. This was the first direct evidence that stars are scattered across space and move independently, and are not attached to a single crystal sphere around the Earth.

On 31 December 1719 Flamsteed died, and on 9 February 1720 Halley was appointed as the second Astronomer Royal (a post he held alongside his professorship in Oxford) by King George I, who had ascended the throne in 1714. Now 63, the first thing he had to do was refurbish the Royal Greenwich Observatory, which had been stripped of its instruments and furniture by Flamsteed's widow, who claimed them as part of his estate. Halley received a grant of £500 for the refurbishment, so the widow Flamsteed must have been a pretty thorough house-clearer. Halley might have been expected to settle down to a quiet old age as the grand old man of British science (especially after Newton died, in 1727); but not a bit of it. As well as continuing to observe phenomena such as nebulae (fuzzy patches of light on the sky, some now known to be clusters of stars or other galaxies) and variable stars, in 1722 he began work on a project to map the changing position of the Moon against the background stars over an 18-year period. (This period is called the saros, and is the cycle of motions through which the relative motions of the

Earth, Moon and Sun pass, bringing them back to the same positions with respect to one another every 18 years.) Halley's aim was to establish a technique for determining position at sea from observations of the Moon; he did not expect to live to complete the task, but he did. The observations were never used in navigation, but this does not diminish the skill with which they were made by the elderly astronomer. The key to navigation at sea turned out to be the development of accurate portable chronometers by John Harrison (no relation to Halley's former lieutenant!), who actually visited Halley at Greenwich in 1728 to discuss the problem with him.

Although his wife died on 30 January 1736 (the exact cause is not known) and Halley suffered a stroke at about the same time, leaving him with a slight paralysis in his right hand, he remained active as an observer almost until his death, on 14 January 1742, a few weeks after his 85th birthday. This came at the end of a short illness and gradual loss of strength. We are told that he died while sitting in a comfortable chair, shortly after enjoying a glass of wine.

Halley's later years had been quite comfortable financially, even though (as Flamsteed had rightly pointed out) the income from the post of Astronomer Royal was small. He still had his Oxford post (although towards the end of his life this was in effect a sinecure), and benefited in 1729 from a visit to Greenwich by Queen Caroline (the wife of George II, whom Halley had met in Hanover, and who had succeeded his father in 1727). The queen was intrigued to learn of Halley's former career as the Master and Commander of a king's ship, and that he had served in that capacity for more than three years. At the time, three years in command qualified the officer for a pension of half-pay. Queen Caroline ensured that Halley received his naval pension until his death. He was buried, alongside Mary, in the churchyard at Lee, close to the Observatory. In 1854 the original tombstone was moved to the Observatory and set into a wall there.

Afterword

Halley's fame, and his position in the popular imagination, was ensured nearly seventeen years after his death, when the comet now known by his name returned as he had predicted. Halley himself had been aware that the date he gave for the return, 1758, was only approximate, because the orbit of the comet is constantly being disturbed by the gravitational influence of the planets, notably the giant Jupiter. Its return was actually first seen by a German farmer and amateur astronomer, Georg Palitzsch, on Christmas Day 1758, but astronomers give the date of the return as 1759, counting from its closest approach to the Sun (perihelion) on 13 April that year. As we have seen, the success of Halley's prediction, based on Newton's theory of gravity and laws of mechanics as spelled out in the *Principia*, changed our view of the Universe for ever.

But Halley's posthumous contributions to science weren't finished with the return of 'his' comet. In 1761, the transit of Venus across the face of the Sun was observed, using the techniques he had spelled out back in 1716, from a total of sixty-two observing stations. A similar number of observing stations monitored the transit of 1769, and the combined results of all these measurements were used to work out the distance from the Earth to the Sun. The result, 153 million km, is commendably close to the modern value of 149.6 million km. Halley thus made his last major contribution to astronomy twenty-seven years after he died.

What Halley never knew, of course, is what comets are made of, how big they are and where they come from. We now know that these objects are 'dirty snowballs', largely composed of different kinds of ice (including frozen water, frozen carbon dioxide and frozen methane) with lumps of rock and dust embedded in them. They are quite small – Halley's Comet itself, photographed by the Giotto probe during its passage through the inner Solar System is 1986, is an irregular potato-shaped lump roughly 16 km long and 8 km across, about the size of the island of Manhattan. Comets become visible as spectacular heavenly objects only when they approach the Sun close enough for the Sun's heat to evaporate some of the icy material, making a tenuous cloud which streams out behind the comet in a long tail that reflects sunlight.

Comets are almost certainly bits of material left over from the birth of the Solar System, some 5 billion years ago. They are thought to form a huge cloud around the entire Solar System, called the Öpik–Oort Cloud, reaching literally halfway to the nearest star, a hundred thousand times farther from the Sun than we are. There may be more comets in the cloud than there are stars in the Milky Way Galaxy – hundreds of billions of them. From time to time some of the comets in the cloud are disturbed, probably by the gravitational influence of a nearby star, and fall in towards the Sun. Many of these whip round the Sun and disappear into the depths of space again; a few, like Halley's Comet, are captured by the gravity of Jupiter and shifted into elliptical orbits around the Sun which bring them on repeated journeys through the inner Solar System every few decades or centuries. Just occasionally, one of these objects may strike the Earth – the impact of a large comet is the front-runner as the explanation for the death of the dinosaurs, some 65 million years ago.

All this would have fascinated Halley. It's strange that somebody who is a household name can still be one of the most underrated scientists of all time. Although highly regarded in his own lifetime, for two hundred years following his death Halley's achievements were largely overshadowed by those of Newton, when in any other generation he would have stood out as the greatest astronomer – perhaps the greatest scientist – of his day. As for his wider activities, any fictional account of a hero who solved the mysteries of the Universe, took time off to command a king's ship, and served as inventor, diplomat and spy on the side might seem just a little implausible, combining the best attributes of Stephen Hawking, Horatio Hornblower, Thomas Edison and James Bond. But Halley was for real. We hope we have done a little to redress the balance as far as the public perception of this remarkable man is concerned.

A brief history of science

All science is either physics or stamp collecting.

Ernest Rutherford

c. 2000 BC	First phase of construction at Stonehenge, an early observatory.
430 BC	Democritus teaches that everything is made of atoms.
c. 330 BC	Aristotle teaches that the Universe is made of concentric spheres, centred on the Earth.
300 BC	Euclid gathers together and writes down the mathematical knowledge of his time.
265 BC	Archimedes discovers his principle of buoyancy while having a bath.
c. 235 BC	Eratosthenes of Cyrene calculates the size of the Earth with commendable accuracy.
AD 79	Pliny the Elder dies while

	studying an eruption of Mount Vesuvius.
400	The term 'chemistry' is used for the first time, by scholars in Alexandria.
c. 1020	Alhazen, the greatest scientist of the so-called Dark Ages, explains the workings of lenses and parabolic mirrors.
1054	Chinese astronomers observe a supernova; the remnant is visible today as the Crab Nebula.
1490	Leonardo da Vinci studies the capillary action of liquids.
1543	In his book *De revolutionibus*, Nicolaus Copernicus places the Sun, not the Earth, at the centre of the Solar System. Andreas Vesalius studies human anatomy in a scientific way.
c. 1550	The reflecting telescope, and later the refracting telescope,

	pioneered by Leonard Digges.
1572	Tycho Brahe observes a supernova.
1580	Prospero Alpini realizes that plants come in two sexes.
1596	Botanical knowledge is summarized in John Gerrard's *Herbal*.
1608	Hans Lippershey's invention of a refracting telescope is the first for which there is firm evidence.
1609–19	Johannes Kepler publishes his laws of planetary motion.
1610	Galileo Galilei observes the moons of Jupiter through a telescope.
1628	William Harvey publishes his discovery of the circulation of the blood.
1643	Mercury barometer invented by Evangelista Torricelli.
1656	Christiaan Huygens correctly identifies the rings of Saturn,

and invents the pendulum clock.

1662   The law relating the pressure and volume of a gas discovered by Robert Boyle, and named after him.

1665   Robert Hooke describes living cells.

1668   A functional reflecting telescope is made by Isaac Newton, unaware of Digges's earlier work.

1673   Antony van Leeuwenhoeck reports his discoveries with the microscope to the Royal Society.

1675   Ole Roemer measures the speed of light by timing eclipses of the moons of Jupiter.

1683   Van Leeuwenhoeck observes bacteria.

1687   Publication of Newton's

Principia, which includes his law of gravitation.

1705   Edmond Halley publishes his prediction of the return of the comet that now bears his name.

1737   Carl Linnaeus publishes his classification of plants.

1749   Georges Louis Leclerc, Comte de Buffon, defines a species in the modern sense.

1758   Halley's Comet returns, as predicted.

1760   John Michell explains earthquakes.

1772   Carl Scheele discovers oxygen; Joseph Priestley independently discovers it two years later.

1773   Pierre de Laplace begins his work on refining planetary orbits. When asked by Napoleon why there was no mention of God in his scheme, Laplace replied, 'I have no need of that hypothesis.'

1783   John Michell is the first person to suggest the existence of 'dark stars' – now known as black holes.

1789   Antoine Lavoisier publishes a table of thirty-one chemical elements.

1796   Edward Jenner carries out the first inoculation, against smallpox.

1798   Henry Cavendish determines the mass of the Earth.

1802   Thomas Young publishes his first paper on the wave theory of light.
         Jean-Baptiste Lamarck invents the term 'biology'.

1803   John Dalton proposes the atomic theory of matter.

1807   Humphrey Davy discovers sodium and potassium, and goes on to find several other elements.

1811	Amedeo Avogadro proposes the law that gases contain equal numbers of molecules under the same conditions.
1816	Augustin Fresnel develops his version of the wave theory of light.
1826	First photograph from nature obtained by Nicéphore Niépce.
1828	Friedrich Wöhler synthesizes an organic compound (urea) from inorganic ingredients.
1830	Publication of the first volume of Charles Lyell's *Principles of Geology*.
1831	Michael Faraday and Joseph Henry discover electromagnetic induction. Charles Darwin sets sail on the *Beagle*.
1837	Louis Agassiz coins the term 'ice age' (*die Eiszeit*).
1842	Christian Doppler describes

the effect that now bears his name.

1849   Hippolyte Fizeau measures the speed of light to within 5 per cent of the modern value.

1851   Jean Foucault uses his eponymous pendulum to demonstrate the rotation of the Earth.

1857   Publication of Darwin's *Origin of Species*. Coincidentally, Gregor Mendel begins his experiments with pea breeding.

1864   James Clerk Maxwell formulates equations describing all electric and magnetic phenomena, and shows that light is an electromagnetic wave.

1868   Jules Janssen and Norman Lockyer identify helium from its lines in the Sun's spectrum.

1871   Dmitri Mendeleyev predicts

that 'new' elements will be found to fit the gaps in his periodic table.

1887 Experiment carried out by Albert Michelson and Edward Morley finds no evidence for the existence of an 'aether'.

1895 X-rays discovered by Wilhelm Röntgen. Sigmund Freud begins to develop psychoanalysis.

1896 Antoine Becquerel discovers radioactivity.

1897 Electron identified by Joseph Thomson.

1898 Marie and Pierre Curie discover radium.

1900 Max Planck explains how electromagnetic radiation is absorbed and emitted as quanta. Various biologists rediscover Medel's principles of genetics and heredity.

1903 First powered and controlled

flight in an aircraft heavier than air, by Orville Wright.

1905   Einstein's special theory of relativity published.

1908   Hermann Minkowski shows that the special theory of relativity can be elegantly explained in geometrical terms if time is the fourth dimension.

1909   First use of the word 'gene', by Wilhelm Johannsen.

1912   Discovery of cosmic rays by Victor Hess. Alfred Wegener proposes the idea of continental drift, which led in the 1960s to the theory of plate tectonics.

1913   Discovery of the ozone layer by Charles Fabry.

1914   Ernest Rutherford discovers the proton, a name he coins in 1919.

1915   Einstein presents his general theory of relativity to the

	Prussian Academy of Sciences.
1916	Karl Schwarzschild shows that the general theory of relativity predicts the existence of what are now called black holes.
1919	Arthur Eddington and others observe the bending of starlight during a total eclipse of the Sun, and so confirm the accuracy of the general theory of relativity. Rutherford splits the atom.
1923	Louis de Broglie suggests that electrons can behave as waves.
1926	Enrico Fermi and Paul Dirac discover the statistical rules which govern the behaviour of quantum particles such as electrons.
1927	Werner Heisenberg develops the uncertainty principle.
1928	Alexander Fleming discovers penicillin.

1929	Edwin Hubble discovers that the Universe is expanding.
1930s	Linus Pauling explains chemistry in terms of quantum physics.
1932	Neutron discovered by James Chadwick.
1937	Grote Reber builds the first radio telescope.
1942	First controlled nuclear reaction achieved by Enrico Fermi and others.
1940s	George Gamow, Ralph Alpher and Robert Herman develop the Big Bang theory of the origin of the Universe.
1948	Richard Feynman extends quantum theory by developing quantum electrodynamics.
1951	Francis Crick and James Watson work out the helix structure of DNA, using X-ray results obtained by Rosalind Franklin.

1957	Fred Hoyle, together with William Fowler and Geoffrey and Margaret Burbidge, explains how elements are synthesized inside stars. The laser is devised by Gordon Gould. Launch of first artificial satellite, *Sputnik 1*.
1960	Jacques Monod and Francis Jacob identify messenger RNA.
1961	First part of the genetic code cracked by Marshall Nirenberg.
1963	Discovery of quasars by Maarten Schmidt.
1964	W.D. Hamilton explains altruism in terms of what is now called sociobiology.
1965	Arno Penzias and Robert Wilson discover the cosmic background radiation left over from the Big Bang.

1967   Discovery of the first pulsar by Jocelyn Bell.

1979   Alan Guth starts to develop the inflationary model of the very early Universe.

1988   Scientists at Caltech discover that there is nothing in the laws of physics that forbids time travel.

1995   Top quark identified.

1996   Tentative identification of evidence of primitive life in a meteorite believed to have originated on Mars.